The School Fair

Story by Lorraine Marwood

Illustrations by Rachel Tonkin

Luke and his friend Andrew
had been waiting for this day
for a long time.
Today they were going
to the school fair.
They had been saving
their allowance.

"I might find another race car
for my set," said Luke.

"I hope I can find some more books
about wild animals," said Andrew.

"You boys can go on ahead of me,"
said Luke's mom,
as they walked onto the school grounds.

"Let's go to that stall, first,"
said Luke,
looking over at a big balloon.

Luke and Andrew ran toward
the big balloon.

Toys

Books

5

Andrew stopped to look
at the books.

Luke went to the table
that had all sorts of toys on it.
There were lots of children
looking at the toys.

Luke saw a dark green race car.
"That's the one I want," he said.

But another boy picked it up first.
He held it up
and started looking at it.

"Oh, **no**," said Luke. "I was too late."

He was just turning to go,
when he saw the boy
put the car back.
Luke rushed over and picked it up.
He gave it to the woman
behind the table.

"I want to buy this car, please,"
he said.

Luke put his hand into his pocket
to get the money.
But his pocket was empty!
He put his hand into his other pocket.
That was empty, too!

Luke had to think fast.
The woman behind the table
was looking at him.

"Could you keep
the car for me, please?"
he asked her.
"Just for a little while?
I need to find my money."

Luke didn't know what to do.

Then he saw Andrew.
"I've lost my money," he said.
"Could you lend me some?"

Andrew shook his head.
"I'm sorry," he said.
"I've just bought two books
and I don't have any money left."

BOOKS BOOKS

BOOKS BOOK

Luke felt so sad.
He walked slowly back to the toy stall.
He was just about to tell the woman
that he couldn't buy the car,
when suddenly he saw his mother.

"Do you want this, Luke?" she asked.

"My **money**!" said Luke.
"I remember now.
I put my money in your bag.
Thanks, Mom!
Now I can pay for that race car!"

And he rushed over and bought it.